Captive
Notions

Captive
Notions

Concise Commentaries
on the Commonplace

by
John E. King

Little Philosophies Press
Seattle, Washington, USA

Published 2005.
Little Philosophies Press, LLC
1001 Fourth Avenue, Suite 3200
Seattle, Washington 98154, USA
Website: www.captivenotions.com
E-mail address: publisher@captivenotions.com.
Printed in the United States of America.

09 08 07 06 05   1 2 3 4 5

ISBN: 0-9760850-5-4

Publisher's Cataloging-in-Publication Data
(Provided by Quality Books, Inc.)

King, John E., 1941-
Captive notions : concise commentaries on the
commonplace / by John E. King
p. cm.
Includes index.
LCCN 2004097058
ISBN 0-9760850-5-4

1. Aphorisms and apothegms.   I. Title.

PS3611.I5786C36 2005   818'.602
                                     QBI04-700552

This book is printed on acid-free paper.

To my children

*Paradoxes are useful
to attract attention to ideas.*
— Bishop Mandell Creighton

*This delivering of knowledge in distinct and disjointed
aphorisms doth leave the wit of man more free to turn and
toss, and to make use of that which is so delivered
to more several purposes and applications.*
— Sir Francis Bacon

Brevity is the soul of wit.
— William Shakespeare

Contents

> *Limited in his nature, infinite*
> *in his desires, man is a fallen god*
> *who remembers heaven.*
> — Alphonse de Lamartine

> *Other sins find their vent in the*
> *accomplishment of evil deeds, whereas pride*
> *lies in wait for good deeds to destroy them.*
> — Saint Augustine

When prosperity comes,
do not use all of it.
— Confucius

Some people will never learn anything,
for this reason, because they
understood everything too soon.
— Alexander Pope

Nothing will ever be attempted,
if all possible objections
must be first overcome.
— Samuel Johnson

When children appear, we justify
all our weaknesses, compromises, snobberies,
by saying: "It's for the children's sake."
- Anton Chekhov

A merry heart
doeth good like a medicine.
— Proverbs

It requires an impartial man to make
a good historian; but it is the partial
and one-sided who hunt out the materials.
— John Dalberg, 1ˢᵗ Baron Acton

Truth must necessarily be
stranger than fiction; for fiction is
the creation of the human mind
and therefore congenial to it.
— G. K. Chesterton

May you have a lawsuit
in which you know you are in the right.
— Gypsy curse

Ere you consult your fancy,
consult your purse.
— Benjamin Franklin

Democracy becomes a government
of bullies tempered by editors.
— Ralph Waldo Emerson

Power is so apt to be insolent,
and liberty to be saucy, that they
are very seldom upon good terms.
— George Savile, 1st Marquis of Halifax

To establish oneself in the world,
one does all one can
to seem established there already.
— François, Duc de La Rochefoucauld

*Love is a sport in which
the hunter must contrive
to have the quarry in pursuit.*
— Alphonse Kerr

Better be quarreling than lonesome.
— Irish proverb

*We work not only to produce
but to give value to time.*
— Eugène Delacroix

Acknowledgments

My thanks to all who over the years have provided support and guidance to me in the writing and publication of this book. Special thanks to my editors, Sally Hayman and Kathleen Florio; my designer, Diane Pettengill; my website designers, Claudia Mazzie-Ballheim and Brandon Ballheim; Carol Kaiser, who has counseled on a variety of editorial and design matters; Ted King, who has advised on assorted design and publication questions; Charlie Greenleaf and Maureen Rooney, who have offered encouragement and thoughtful suggestions over many years; and Wyatt King, Cabell King, and Carrington and Garrett Cunnington, who have provided inspiration and insight as the project has evolved. My gratitude for their contributions is only enhanced by recognition that, as ultimate decisions regarding content, style, and other matters have been mine, so also is responsibility for errors and misjudgments.

J.E.K.

Preface

For more than a decade I have jotted down on scraps of paper observations from daily life that have struck me as ironic, or as otherwise noteworthy but seldom noted. Sometimes triggered by a news item, a passage in a book, a casual conversation, or the like, they have more often emerged unaccountably from some ripple in the everyday stream of consciousness. Perceptions with a clear ring of truth have routinely mingled with questionable hypotheses.

I have thoroughly enjoyed the pastime. It has afforded the opportunity to explore ironies and idiosyncrasies of everyday life, common threads among seemingly unrelated situations, public policy implications of ordinary happenings, and the richness of the English language. The exercise has helped me make sense of life.

There have been minor inconveniences, such as occasional interruptions of other activities and rare bouts of insomnia induced by groping for just the right words or sentence structure. Most frustrating have been struggles to remember observations — especially more than one at a time — arising when I have been unable to record them in the moment. In those circumstances, some have escaped my net.

Over time, the scraps of paper bearing the notations have found their way into stacks on tabletops and in desk drawers. At some point I decided to cull and edit them with a view to publication, tasks which have proven both exacting and pleasurable. The result is *Captive Notions* — so named because it contains the ones that didn't get away.

My aim has been to craft each selected observation into an aphorism, "a tersely phrased statement of a truth or opinion." (The American Heritage Dictionary, 4th ed.) The book's entries are all brief: most are a single sentence — none more than two — while some are in the form of definitions. Whether a particular selection is a truth or an opinion I leave to the judgment of the reader. With allowances for occasional flights of whimsy, all are heartfelt. Some deliver their messages plainly, others indirectly: if one yields a quick "aha" and another elicits reflection and pondering of implications, both will have done their work.

Captive Notions deals with matters affecting not only people's personal lives, in chapters like "Ambition," "Character," and "Lifestyles," but also their civic lives, in chapters such as "Economics," "History," and "Politics and Democracy." This mingling of observations on personal and social issues reflects a premise of the book that people's daily lives are as affected by matters of public as of private concern.

While the chapters of the book generally treat related themes together, each aphorism is self-contained. This allows for perusal cover-to-cover, by chapters, or at random, and by readers on the move as well as at leisure. Whatever your circumstances and preferences, I hope you will find *Captive Notions* a congenial companion and a stimulus for both solitary musing and thoughtful conversation.

J.E.K.

Editorial Note

For economy of expression, the text of *Captive Notions* generally limits references to male and female genders to one or the other in specific instances (using them about equally). Unless the context indicates otherwise, a reference to either gender includes the other.

Ambition

To ask too much of oneself
is to deny the talents of others.

He who strives for too much
accomplishes too little.

If you want to do everything,
you will be seen as willing to do anything.

If you're not moving forward, you're moving backward. Those moving forward will see to that.

⚜

One who relishes doing the impossible will find ways to make things so.

⚜

As many as the Horatio Alger mythology has inspired, at least as many has it seduced.

⚜

Even those who will contribute the most must commonly contend for the opportunity.

⚜

Opportunity is a birthright into which one must commonly muscle one's way.

Opportunity is a thing you must have
in order to prove you deserve it.

❦

A land of opportunity enables
the widespread distribution of elitism.

❦

A person of diverse talents
risks their feuding.

❦

Seek to use all your talents
at the risk of using none.

❦

For every talent there's a pigeonhole.

❦

Mediocrity is emboldened
by the multitude of its legions.

❦

In life as in sports, no amount of talent
makes up for being out of position.

❦

Talent has value only in the estimation of others.

❦

A leader arranges success,
whoever's in charge.

❦

Natural leader: a person whose instincts lead her
to the right pond in which to become a big fish.

❦

Many a putative leader serves chiefly as a catalyst
for the ambitions of his cohorts.

Success lies in placing oneself
where progress is heading.

As important to our success in life as what we are
is what we think of what we are.

Life is like a crossword puzzle:
the more you help yourself, the more it helps you.

When a person is elevated too quickly,
his head is liable to keep rising.

No matter how important you are, you are far less important to just about everyone else than he is.

❧

The perfectionist hones the tools of her own undoing.

❧

One who insists on doing a perfect job will gravitate to modest tasks.

❧

Ambition for the great deflects from accomplishment of the good.

❧

Many a life is spent attempting to prove its worth.

❧

Some people expend so much energy
creating their potential they have
little left for realizing it.

❧

Tilting at windmills
leaves the real dragons unslain.

❧

The brilliant best all but their demons.

❧

The race is to the swift and their handlers.

❧

The American dream allows everyone
to aspire to an ideal upbringing.

❧

America is a land of opportunity —
for the next generation.

⚜

It is a measure of a society what a person
can make of herself not only from a humble
beginning but also from a humble middle.

⚜

If at first you don't succeed, try, try again.
Then try a different game.

⚜

In the big leagues, to survive is to succeed.

⚜

Most idealists don't know any better.

⚜

You can fail in the service of God
only by getting in your own way.

❧

It is a rare attainment that carries with it
no potential for new annoyances.

❧

Life is a game in which the team that just scored
customarily remains on offense.

❧

The mighty seldom fall
to the depths of the mightless.

❧

An advantage lost is a disadvantage;
a disadvantage surmounted, an advantage.

An illusory advantage is a disadvantage.

❧

Advantage compounds.

❧

Character

Honesty reveals our flaws,
but tends to upstage them.

One acquires depth
from being in a hole.

Reality is best faced
only after ideals are entrenched.

Small acts of courage attract; great ones oft repel.

Who we are is largely a matter of
what we are prepared to do.

As indicative of character as how you react
to your own adversity is how you react
to others' successes.

Character reveals itself in the partisanship
of one with no dog in the fight.

Heredity may provide a talent,
but environment channels it toward
self-indulgence or service to humanity.

A virtue markedly either advances
or impedes one's temporal interests.

꧁❀꧂

A close personal attachment
tends to either bolster or strain a person's
commitment to her principles.

꧁❀꧂

A vice unacknowledged is a vice forever.

꧁❀꧂

There are no bargains in vices.

꧁❀꧂

The better one's decisions,
the fewer required.

꧁❀꧂

A bad decision clears the way for a good one;
indecision paves the way for more indecision.

❧

In matters of heart and soul,
all are entrepreneurs.

❧

A lie is more easily lived than told.

❧

As the devil at large is attractive,
the demon within is seductive.

❧

Souls are more often sold for luxuries
than for necessities.

❧

The spirit animates the conscience.

⚜

Behind every generous person
is another generous person.

⚜

Live in the moment:
abandon prejudices more than
a generation out of date.

⚜

She who hides from others
hides more from herself.

⚜

Personality thrives on small vices.

⚜

A self-starter is usually fired
by a donated ignition.

❧

Instincts of survival beget habits
of domination — or of servitude.

❧

The self-effacing commonly hope
to be given credit for not taking it.

❧

Patience is nurtured by forgetfulness.

❧

Defining a person's worth
solely in financial terms tends to be
especially apt when applied to
one who does so.

Attitudes are the channels
through which abilities flow.

❦

The qualities in ourselves
we most prize are commonly those
for which we're least responsible.

❦

Perfection: the excellence of fantasy.

❦

Guilt is an overpaid governor.

❦

Worry tends to rattle around the head
until finding a notion to cling to.

❦

As a worthy servant
may serve an unworthy master, a worthy effort
may serve an unworthy cause.

We live the lives we create for ourselves,
albeit seldom by our own scripts or rules.

Self-discipline:
doing what doesn't come naturally.

An ounce of judgment is worth a pound of effort.

A heart in the right place is easily moved.

Economics

The greatest rewards in the economic chain
accrue to the links nearest the lock.

❦

The trickle-down theory is undermined
by a streambed of sponges.

❦

For every overpaid executive
there's a worthwhile cause underserved.

Many an executive compensation committee
has replaced keeping up with the Joneses
with keeping up with the Rockefellers.

❦

The myriad explosions that drive the engine of
the economy are no less idiosyncratic for seeming
rather uniform and predictable in the aggregate.

❦

Money: a universal medium
for the disguise of worth.

❦

Every cost is ultimately someone's wage or profit.

❦

Fears of deflation have conferred on
the raising of prices an aura of patriotism.

A cost rises in proportion
to the number of people sharing it.

❧

A price rises to greet a subsidy.

❧

A subsidy to one's customers has the effect
of a subsidy to oneself, without
apparent compromise of one's commitment
to the principles of the market.

❧

An industry will expand indefinitely
to absorb a subsidy.

❧

Abundance: the product of those who supply
more than they demand.

Consumers thrive on simplicity,
suppliers on complexity.

❧

Commerce thrives on celebrations.

❧

It is a genius of capitalism
to place on most of its participants just about
as much pressure as they can bear.

❧

As it exploits and harnesses vices,
capitalism also fine-tunes them.

❧

Interdependence is a censor
embedded in capitalism.

The cause of capitalism flourishes
on the tidiness of its theory.

❦

For all its resemblance to a state of nature,
vibrant capitalism is largely
a creature of benign government.

❦

Incentives beget inequities.

❦

The laws of economics explain all the movements
of money except from those who earn it
to those who help them spend it.

❦

Philanthropy is capitalism's crowning glory,
the need for philanthropy its Achilles' heel.

Individualism multiplies the market
by dividing the marketplace.

❦

It's the market's imperfections
that treat its participants well.

❦

Of any social movement likely to increase overall
consumer demand, business is a natural ally,
its apparent apprehension customarily portending
not obstruction but rather guidance into
the most manageable and lucrative channels.

❦

A modern economy aims to support educating
the populace well enough to desire and afford the
assorted wares it offers, but not so well
as to prefer doing without them.

An expanding economy is a particular
imperative of an inequitable one.

❧

Recessions would be easily weathered
if their burdens were evenly shared.

❧

The economy is a banquet at which there are
routinely more guests than places at the table.

❧

Hardship lies in everyone's needing a piece
of an economy that doesn't need everyone.

❧

Hardship keeps the American dream alive.

❧

The marginally employed
are the shock absorbers of capitalism.

❦

Many who tout the wonders
of a free-market economy nevertheless
deny its capability to make major productive tasks
palatable to its labor force.

❦

Severance pay bears witness
to defects in the employment market.

❦

Business pays homage to the invisible hand
while seeking to escape its grasp.

❦

The invisible hand has greasy fingers.

Beware an appeal to parity from an entity
permitted to choose its own peers.

❦

The middle class is the one that has
just about what it needs.

❦

In stimulating the economy,
the government routinely ensures
that a sizable proportion of wealth
is unearned.

❦

Inflation makes investments of indulgences.

❦

An orderly securities market is one from which
the experts can exit before it plummets.

Commerce invariably improves lives —
and invariably disproportionately.

❦

The first principle of social welfare in America is
that it not detract from the making of fortunes.

❦

Inflationary psychology:
that which ensures that low mortgage rates
result in higher housing prices.

❦

Middlemen thrive on others' windfalls.

❦

Technological advance: an event tending to
disperse economic power among consumers
and concentrate it among providers.

A celebrity society
creates a feudal economy.

❧

A venerable institution is only as reliable
as its latest stewards.

❧

In making available a single word
for both singular and plural
of the second-person pronoun,
the English language has
conferred a singular benefit
on the advertising industry.

❧

An insurer thrives on the prospect of that
of which it abhors the occurrence.

❧

The health care industry
has acquired much of its
immense share of the economy
by keeping those who pay
for most of its services well apart
from most of those who receive them.

❦

Most health insurance protects not only
against catastrophe but also against
improvidence and inconvenience.

❦

Bonanza:
that which customarily characterizes
an industry providing a service as to which
the populace is committed to both
untrammeled private enterprise
and universal participation.

❦

An American professional sports league is to
its host cities like a fickle lady of high station,
routinely keeping a handful of suitors
in the wings in case one of the first-stringers
fails to treat her and her retinue in the style
to which they have become accustomed.

⚜

If a conspiracy would be unlawful, try a merger.

⚜

Merger: a process by which a going concern
becomes a write-off.

⚜

The most bountiful investments
flow from charitable donations.

⚜

Many a profitable undertaking
is routinely subsidized by charity.

❦

The most compelling charities are commonly
among the least conspicuous.

❦

We all depend on the farmer,
who depends on God.

❦

Education

Education diminishes one's capacity for boredom,
but makes it less likely.

A superior education should enable one
to either earn handsomely or live frugally.

All the genius a person can muster
is in service to his intuition.

Students learn what teachers
want to learn more of.

❧

Those who can, do.
Those who believe others can also, teach.

❧

To study is to seek more to enjoy.

❧

Curiosity reveals false gods and true heroes.

❧

Knowledge is the toy of the intellect.

❧

For an incentive to learn facts, listen to opinions.

Education is an entrée into
a more sophisticated set of biases.

⁂

Reading is an adventure,
research an adventure with a mission.

⁂

Learning is play.
Being accountable for knowing is work.

⁂

It is a special fruit of education
to render the useful enjoyable.

⁂

No sphere of knowledge is more
randomly acquired than that of oneself.

Many a fine student knows little of herself.

In mastering a subject,
beware of being mastered by it.

The most important part of education
is learning what to learn.

The most valuable lessons
are those deliberately not taught.

To entrench a social condition,
formalize training to cope with it.

A hazard of our system of higher education
is a tendency to encourage us to focus
on distinctions among ourselves.

❧

Over-education enlightens to the point
one's feet no longer touch the ground.

❧

Learning, like loving, may be done not wisely
but too well.

❧

High marks suggest good scholarship;
perfect marks suggest fear of failure.

❧

Experience: the phase of education
for which one aims to be paid.

The college admissions process:
a ritual for democratizing elitism.

꙳

Many a prestigious school more commonly
touts its raw material than its value added.

꙳

College: a place that for many
requires the self-discipline
to learn pretty much whatever
captures their fancies.

꙳

Live and learn. Live longer and forget.

꙳

Enterprise

Everything one wants is within the power
of someone to provide.

The early bird sets the agenda.

One is customarily better served by a
predisposition to place an advertisement
than to answer one.

Innovation lies in exploiting one's inklings.

❧

As long as life is difficult,
opportunity will abound.

❧

An ounce of initiative
yields a pound of opportunity.

❧

Many a step outside the box
is into another one.

❧

That initiative works best that
stimulates the initiative of others.

❧

Entrepreneurship: the crown jewel of capitalism.

A happy entrepreneur is one who makes
a business of what she does best.

The best entrepreneurship
is an extension of craftsmanship.

Entrepreneurship:
a struggle positioned for a windfall.

Entrepreneurship:
a quest to tap a hidden cornucopia.

Successful entrepreneurship transforms
a supplicant into a potentate.

❀

The hard work of life is preparing
for strokes of good fortune.

❀

Luck is inevitable.
The skill lies in making it happen to you.

❀

A land of opportunity looks a lot like
a land of selective windfalls.

❀

Much of the lore of capitalism is
built around the most likely to succeed
who don't and the least likely who do.

A big risk lurks in avoidance of small ones.

❧

To unduly fear a bad bargain
is to seldom get a good one.

❧

You can't prove your worth without being tried.

❧

A virtue is most rewarded
when tied to a skill.

❧

One person's incentive is another's windfall.

❧

One windfall becomes a precedent for another.

Success is most often achieved by redefining it.

The backbone of one's enterprise
is others' necessity for livelihoods.

Many a fortune is acquired
making others feel useful.

Nearly every fortune is made with the
material aid of someone who doesn't make one.

The most consistently important ingredient
in the success of a challenging enterprise
is companionship.

Many a promoter thrives
on her customers serving one another.

❧

The essence of building a business
is building barriers to competing with it.

❧

More patronage is acquired from habit
than from decision.

❧

You can fool all of the people some of the time
and some of the people all of the time —
ample for good living.

❧

The rewards of enterprise
are routinely too small or too great.

Financial rewards come to those who make
themselves needed by people who are not needy.

❦

To readily acquire money requires dealing with
those well positioned to part with it.

❦

A fortune is most often made
helping someone else make a greater one.

❦

Small fortunes are made by providing expertise,
large ones by making it obsolete.

❦

Wealth lies in finding an ample niche
with a narrow entrance.

Prosperity lies in getting in the way of money.

❧

Most money is made by doing more of the same.

❧

Intellectualism tends to distract
from making money because
most of the latter is in the execution.

❧

A culture that honors taking risks
will contrive to maintain hazards.

❧

Making money:
the old-fashioned way of acquiring it.

❧

The fruits of industry and of good fortune
are indistinguishable to the naked eye.

✧

Salesmanship:
the art of creating and exploiting whims.

✧

Everyone occasionally does something irrational.
A salesperson's job is to be there when it happens.

✧

Investing: the means by which a person
puts the engines of civilization to work for her.

✧

Investment aims to create wealth,
speculation to throw a net over it.

Investing for the long term ensures one's adviser
is well paid before she's accountable.

※

As long as compounding seems a miracle,
the investment profession
will claim for itself the role of magician.

※

Compounding seems distinctly less of a miracle
when you're counting on it.

※

The profits of today include royalties
on the ingenuity of the ages.

※

Family, Childhood, and Youth

The hazards of one's life
are infinitesimal compared with those
that might have precluded it altogether.

Whatever we think of our ancestry,
we wouldn't have had it any other way.

The black sheep of yesteryear
are today's jewels of genealogy.

❧

The inbred are full of themselves.

❧

We need families to define the limits
of our best intentions.

❧

The sins of the fathers most visited upon the sons
are the ones the fathers claimed were virtues.

❧

Many would haggle with a saint
to lavish upon an ingrate.

❧

The lifestyle of the parent
is the world of the child.

❧

The pretensions of the parents
become the assumptions of the children.

❧

Impress your neighbors at the risk
of confounding your children.

❧

A loving parent is worth any number of pedigrees.

❧

Parenting: society's most important function for
which qualification is routinely taken for granted.

❧

Parenting: an instrumentality for transforming
ordinary impulses into momentous consequences.

※

A parent exercises more influence unwittingly
than nearly anyone else intentionally.

※

A parent is as likely to influence a child
by what she does occasionally
as by what she does repeatedly.

※

It's easy to influence your child,
though seldom just as you intend.

※

Parenting: a discipline that consistently
rewards restraint in the exercise of power.

Parental severity: solving today's small problem by creating tomorrow's big one.

❦

Childhood: the source of most ideas regarding what to do with what we learn as adults.

❦

The child who least anticipates life's hardships becomes best prepared to face them.

❦

The most nurtured become the least dependent.

❦

A child seen and not heard is liable to grow up neither seen nor heard.

❦

It is a bulwark of democracy that quality
in parenting transcends class distinctions.

࿇

In youthful awards lie the seeds of adult elitism.

࿇

Grandchildren give parents a second chance —
this time with the benefit of schooling.

࿇

Health and Nurture

The Lord helps those who help themselves,
in their fashion; those who help others,
in his fashion.

Many a cry for help is made with a snarl.

Empathy:
the universal primary care.

Judgment intrudes where empathy fails.

❧

None soar but that others have launched.

❧

Where a schoolmaster or employer
would drill repeatedly, a physician or dentist
commonly counsels casually.

❧

A person is seldom blamed
for the disabilities of his body,
routinely for those of his mind.

❧

A neurotic tends to be ill in ways hard to forgive.

❧

The more widespread an emotional illness,
the more readily seen as normal.

⋘⋙

Emotional health: an exceptional condition
treated as a cultural norm.

⋘⋙

Mental health professional:
a person with the temerity to tell you
that your most prized qualities
are the most disturbing.

⋘⋙

A disturbing feature of
emotional illness statistics is that
a sizable share of the statistics
are unaware of their inclusion.

⋘⋙

Emotional illness entails the added disability
of tending to be self-aggravating
rather than self-healing.

❧

Denial: a state in which a jolt of reality
is just another obstacle to be overcome.

❧

Illness attacks the organism.
Denial attacks the cure.

❧

Many an evil flows from an illness.

❧

Among the most baffling ailments
are those disguised as competence.

Illnesses we don't understand
we hope to cure by opprobrium.

⚜

Unnecessary precautions add up.

⚜

Offsetting compulsions simulate normality.

⚜

Many an eccentricity
is an earnest attempt at perfection.

⚜

As you get older, you generally
do get better, albeit in part from coping
with what's getting worse.

⚜

History

It is the blessing of each generation to stand on the shoulders of its collective predecessors.

We are all heirs to most of what we have.

Peoples advance slowly, ever with the capacity to squander in a comparative moment sizable portions of their accumulated heritage.

Times change because their ingredients change.

❦

Those who write history make history,
but so do those who write fiction.

❦

Those who write history make history,
and thereby also a measure of the future.

❦

A new generation of something
begins every day.

❦

The empire of one generation
becomes the melting pot of the next.

❦

Time makes rights of privileges.

❦

Denigrating the past is especially annoying
to those still living there.

❦

To belittle the past is to flatter the present.

❦

History is a foil for celebration
of the prejudices of today.

❦

History:
a battlefield on which scholars are the generals,
our sense of ourselves commonly the prize.

❦

To misread history is to err with authority.

❧

The lessons of history are more reliable
than its judgments.

❧

For all its invocation as a rationale for learning
history, avoidance of repeating its mistakes
is but erratically addressed in the teaching of it.

❧

Selectiveness by itself is sufficient
to make history a realm of mythology.

❧

If history is presented disproportionately
through study of its wars, students are liable
to view peacetimes as aberrations.

It is not uncommon
to chastise our collective forebears
for their inability to achieve
for themselves what they
have achieved for us.

❦

The past has the comparative disadvantage
of having improved the present.

❦

The people of tomorrow
will get a kind of world
more deserved by the people of today.

❦

All the world's peoples are ancient,
even if not all yet storied.

❦

Our experience of the world
is as a collection of stories we pick up
and leave off somewhere in the middle.

❦

The rhetoric of one revolution
paves the way for the next.

❦

An age becomes old-fashioned quickly
by dint of its own enlightenment.

❦

Evolution works in mysterious ways:
surely by now one would expect people
to have eyes in the backs of their heads.

❦

Ideas and Their Expression

The mind is the bottleneck
through which experience flows.

⁂

Many an adult conviction
is in thrall to a childish notion.

⁂

The mind is more prone to accept
what it perceives to pre-exist
than what appears to emerge before it.

❦

The more that goes on in a mind,
the more that can go wrong.

❦

The inquiring mind tends to discount
what it already knows.

❦

A fertile imagination
takes a small pleasure on a long ride.

❦

Imagination is economical.
It's the byproducts that are liable to be costly.

Many a mind is changed by being spoken.

❧

The best way to change a mind
is to expand it.

❧

Errors of omission
are the least likely to be corrected.

❧

A little knowledge is a dangerous thing,
but less so than a little opinion.

❧

It is a mark of high civilization
that much of the bullying is intellectual.

❧

Religion celebrates what science explores.

⁂

A scientific discovery is a revelation of God.

⁂

Anticipation of the next work of a great artist
is an inkling of the hope of the devout.

⁂

Animals must find it as hard to fathom humans
as humans do to fathom God.

⁂

Bricks and mortar alone make a city
for people who live by bread alone.

⁂

Ethics: the struggle to value people
by more than what the world
has invested in them.

❧

Fanciful interpretation
is as ancient as holy writ.

❧

Art differs from science in that
its foremost practitioners do things
more differently than similarly.

❧

Professional artist:
a person who does as she pleases
and is accountable for it.

❧

The bread and butter of the avant-garde
of each generation lies in exploiting demand
previously repressed by conflicts
between the sensibilities and impulses
of the immediately preceding one.

❦

Irreverence: the carnival barker of modern art.

❦

Fine thoughts percolate through fine music.

❦

Music: a catalyst for exploration of the soul.

❦

Listen to your own drummer,
but hear the rest of the orchestra.

She who hears a different drummer
is likely to hear several.

❧

He who listens to his own drummer has no union.

❧

One person's detail is another's grand design.

❧

Conventional wisdom:
that which you're either a hero to have challenged
or a fool not to have heeded.

❧

Information age: one in which the omissions
become more material.

❧

The labor of writing
lies in the molding of thinking.

❧

No risk is too great for a fictional character.

❧

Literature puts truth
in the guise of fiction
and thereby fiction in the guise of truth.

❧

Fiction: a medium of versatile deniability.

❧

Subtlety risks rendering appealing
what it sets out to disparage.

❧

Many a bad lesson is learned from a good book.

❧

Drama thrives on conflict, life on harmony.

❧

A happy ending doesn't last forever.

❧

The more obscure the message,
the more influential the critic.

❧

A villain in one story
is likely to be a victim in another.

❧

Movie: a book dressed up to do the town.

Little endures in a culture
that thrives on its countercultures.

❧

The story of America is the experience
of its journalists and moviemakers.

❧

Psychology: literature with shortcuts.

❧

Plagiarist: a person passing off
the work of another as his own who isn't
important enough to rate a ghostwriter.

❧

Illustrations:
soundings through the choppy waters of ideas.

If statistics lie and a picture is worth
a thousand words, beware of graphs.

❦

No logic is so powerful
as a whim whose time has come.

❦

Creativity is demonstrable
only through the recognizable.

❦

Complexity is simplicity undiscovered.

❦

Philosophy converts the known
into the unknown.

❦

All that is brilliant does not illuminate.

⁂

Where there's a myth there's an agenda.

⁂

Follow a contrarian
only who has mastered the consensus.

⁂

A thicket is a forest from within.

⁂

Careful reasoning is routinely employed
to decide among options afforded by intuition.

⁂

We write things down
so that we won't forget them —
and so that we may.

✿

If you are adept with words,
you can afford to be clumsy
at many of the things they describe.

✿

If necessity is the mother of invention,
she's apparently pro-choice.

✿

The Law

The law is distinguished from the sciences
in that its complexity is contrived.

❧

The nobility of its name
enables the law to lure the idealistic
into the tangled byways of its practice.

❧

Law is fascinating. It's the laws that are tedious.

In the otherwise seamless web of the law,
statutes are the stitches.

❧

Litigiousness is but a symptom of that of which
overreaching and mistrust are the causes.

❧

The judicial process treats with exacting precision
the roughhewn creations of the legislative.

❧

Adversary system:
a system for creating adversaries.

❧

Punitive damages:
a lottery designed to be lost.

Evidence is required to prove
what intuition may disprove.

❦

Expertise:
the power to convert opinions into facts.

❦

Judge: a person who usually does what he's told,
but gets to choose by whom.

❦

Settlement: a result all parties contend is wrong
but against which none are willing to bet.

❦

Compromise: a process by which
old half-truths become a new reality.

Wrongdoing: a characterization that exists principally for the purpose of being denied.

❧

More aberrant behavior proceeds from illness than the practical constraints of the law can afford to acknowledge.

❧

Executive clemency: the crème de la crème benefit of having friends in high places.

❧

Contract: an instrument for the production of great harmony or greater discord.

❧

Legal skills: the martial arts of civil combat.

Legalese: a triumph of the comprehensive
over the comprehensible.

❦

"My kingdom for a horse": an early prototype
of a contingent fee arrangement.

❦

Few realizations are more dispiriting
than that justice is unaffordable.

❦

There are two types of successful lawyers:
those for whom zeal is an asset and those
for whom lack of zeal is an asset.

❦

Lawyer:
one who finds a principle in every interest.

The only person less likely
to evoke sympathy than a lawyer who looks out
for his own interest is one who doesn't.

⁂

The very nobility of the law contributes to the
unfavorable impression of the partiality
required of its practice.

⁂

Connect the dots: in an age of 700-page statutes,
the public at large are still presumed
to know the law.

⁂

Lifestyles

Ladies and gentlemen
bear the fruits of prosperity
without the scars of its acquisition.

Many a bad habit was once a good habit.

If you insist on making each day count,
you're liable to stay up late.

The forces of light clash with those of darkness
in the epic daily struggle to get out of bed.

❧

To arouse the body, engage the mind.

❧

The neglectful take comfort in supposing
they are presumed to have better things to do.

❧

Spontaneity thrives on preparation.

❧

The more active one's life,
the more opportunities for Providence
to intervene.

❧

Today is the first day of rest of your life.
Never mind that it may have begun
with an operating loss carryover.

❧

It is of the essence of life to assert oneself.

❧

Play is the work of one's choosing.

❧

Work before you play,
but plan your play before you work.

❧

To play the game is to win.

❧

The game provides the action,
but the context provides most of the drama.

❧

Carpe diem: there's no time like the present
to run off and join a nudist colony.

❧

To spend time is to invest life.

❧

You might as well enjoy life.
You're paying for it.

❧

It becomes increasingly expensive
to recreate simple pleasures.

❧

Wealth buys simple pleasures
in expensive settings.

❦

It is a challenge to the human spirit
to keep the cost of enjoyment from rising faster
than the cost of living.

❦

One is pigeonholed by one's pleasures.

❦

Many a stress is incurred
to accommodate relaxation.

❦

Rest enables the mind to rotate its inventory.

❦

Rest allows God to work unimpeded.

⋘✦⋙

Time just passes. God heals.

⋘✦⋙

Life is a banquet at which
you must ordinarily serve yourself.

⋘✦⋙

"Because it's there":
a rationale for engaging in large challenges
and small indulgences.

⋘✦⋙

Many an inefficiency
is an opportunity for exercise.

⋘✦⋙

A life well lived is full of loose ends.

❦

A good read is a cheap vacation.

❦

Smart people make money.
Really smart people read arcane books
and solve esoteric crossword puzzles.

❦

The garrulous disparage television
because it won't listen.

❦

Laziness:
relaxation with a life of its own.

❦

The surest way to overeat
is to have overeaten previously.

❦

The pathway to portliness
is lined with special occasions.

❦

Pastry: bread spread on butter.

❦

Dieting is such a major preoccupation
because nutrition is such a minor one.

❦

Why does satiety feel more like hunger
than hunger like satiety?

❦

You can live five years behind the times
at half the price.

❦

Putting away childish things is easy.
It's the stuff of youth we try to hang on to.

❦

Many an elaborate technology
is in service to a simple pursuit.

❦

Personal computer: one for which
you're expected to be your own mechanic.

❦

A little money buys quite a lot of happiness;
a lot more buys comparatively little.

Little wonder that humankind, for thousands
of generations anthropologically hard-wired
for consumption with meager prospects,
should race to exploit the modern cornucopia.

❧

Money buys a lot of what is packaged
to look like happiness.

❧

The largest personal expenditures are usually
aimed at acquiring either privacy or company.

❧

The largest expenses
are commonly embedded in assets.

❧

We would give more if we feared less.

The most rewarding attribute of prosperity
is the capability to be generous.

⁂

Currency:
the form of wealth most reluctantly squandered.

⁂

The poor prize a flower as the rich a garden.

⁂

Home is where the garden tools are.

⁂

To live barely within one's means
is so often a necessity
it tends to be seen as an obligation.

⁂

The more money you have,
the more childlike you can afford to be.

❧

Disappointment becomes annoyance
when hope becomes expectation.

❧

Luxury builds a wall around comfort.

❧

The proceeds of fame and fortune
are obliged to flow through
the bottleneck of human frailty.

❧

Wealth buys a right to a lot of idiosyncrasy.

❧

Compared to power over the lives of others,
the other attributes of exceptional wealth
are relatively inconsequential.

❧

Fashion: the means by which
the rich and powerful become beautiful.

❧

If you keep a black cat, it will cross your path.

❧

Humbling it is to discover, alas,
that one's life has been spent in the control group.

❧

The more varied one's life,
the more often a novice.

A habit of procrastination
serves a yen for excitement.

⚜

If you manage your time efficiently enough,
you can eliminate most of what's worth living for.

⚜

Travel broadens. Staying put deepens.

⚜

The best lives seldom consist of the best stories.

⚜

The Media

A free press is for liberty,
a quick press for profit.

❧

A free press is a bastion of liberty.
A concentrated press
is a bastion of a handful
of carefully prescribed liberties.

❧

The major business entities in the economy
tend to consolidate into a number
the major media can conveniently cover.

❦

The more concentrated the media,
the greater the number of taboo topics.

❦

The more fractured the social order,
the more influential the media.

❦

When attitudes are news,
it is easily contrived.

❦

The court of public opinion has lax rules.

The media create an event
by drawing a crowd.

⚜

The media derive influence
from readers' not so much
agreeing with the media's opinions
as supposing that others do.

⚜

The media make the news
by deeming it newsworthy.

⚜

Today's news creates tomorrow's audience.

⚜

The media concentrate the culture.

The public appreciate winners;
the media demand them.

❧

Symbiosis: the relationship between
the media and celebrities.

❧

Popular culture continually reinvents itself
to feed the media's demand for novelty.

❧

A poll transforms a contest of preferences
into a contest of bandwagons.

❧

The influence of a house editorialist
is enhanced by her comparative anonymity.

A derogatory cartoon
is worth a thousand epithets.

⚜

Selectively published
letters to the editor:
an opportunity for supporters
to embellish the publication's
editorial positions and for critics
to unwittingly ensnare themselves.

⚜

Free broadcast licenses:
subsidies for celebrities.

⚜

A sound bite is harmful only if swallowed.

⚜

Radio talk-show host:
the kid who makes the rules
because he owns the ball.

❧

The media enable political demonstrators
to expand the right of free speech
to include a free audience.

❧

A free press confronts a democracy's hierarchies
with its principles.

❧

Journalism isn't just the first draft of history;
it's the most influential.

❧

Politics and Democracy

In a democracy,
your neighbors are your rulers.

In a democracy, not only
are your neighbors your rulers;
the media are their advisers.

If you're offended by what's on television,
you can turn off your set.
But you can't turn off your neighbor's.

❧

The more populous a democracy,
the less autonomous each citizen.

❧

The instruments of civilization are fine-tuned
to retain a semblance of the law of the jungle.

❧

It is a rare cause so inspiring that some won't ask
others to sacrifice for it disproportionately.

❧

America is a nation that continually reinvents
itself in the name of its founders.

America has such faith in itself
that it sees no obstacles to achievement of its
destiny beyond the capability of its
expected immigrants to overcome.

❦

The law affords a safety net for free speech.
The economy is less accommodating.

❦

Within a democracy
there are comparatively few democracies.

❦

A populous democracy is host to myriad empires.

❦

Elections produce followers
more consistently than leaders.

Political debate: an attempt to capture for politics
the drama and theater of sports.

❧

The voters never have all the information
they need to make fully informed choices.
The politicians see to that.

❧

The ignorant can be trampled.
The educated must be manipulated.

❧

Second-class citizen:
one whose vote is easily manipulated.

❧

The lower the voter turnout,
the more influential the extremists.

A representative democracy commonly becomes less so as soon as the representatives make their own rules to govern their deliberations.

⚜

Representative democracy: the right to choose whose lobbyists will be more favorably received.

⚜

Lobbyists fashion democracy into a gaggle of oligarchies.

⚜

Corporate lobbying: a creature meddling in the affairs of its creator.

⚜

Democracy: government of the people, by the people, for the people — in varying proportions.

In a democracy the government
will occasionally do what the people want —
assuming they get organized
and ally themselves with powerful interests.

❧

Democracy is blessed less by wisdom
than by skepticism of pretensions to wisdom.

❧

Progress in a democracy is impeded
less by a shortage of good ideas than by an
orchestrated clutter of well-financed bad ones.

❧

The dominant force in the world of politics
is the status quo.

❧

The will of the people is only as effective
as their capacity to resist its manipulation.

❧

Independence:
the last refuge of personal power.

❧

There's no need to legislate morality.
Legislating against manifestations
of immorality is sufficient.

❧

The forces of liberalism and conservatism
are each the principal activators of the other.

❧

An accumulation of property makes a
conservative; a dispersal of property makes many.

People tend to dislike politics
because it challenges their ideologies.

❧

Political ideology: a distillation of personal
experience the world is invited to share.

❧

Politics: a medium for leveraging
small advantages into large ones.

❧

In politics many a contest is decided
before one side knows there is one.

❧

It is an aim of politics to make policies
comprehensible, insofar as practicable,
only to those whom they favor.

A successful negotiation is one in which
all parties win at the expense of nonparticipants.

❦

Politics expand to fill a vacuum.

❦

Bravo the politician
who can applaud without subsidizing.

❦

It is an art of the politician to routinely reveal
her heading without revealing her destination.

❦

Politician: one who predicts the future
by asking you to trust him.

❦

It's easier to placate a constituency
than to solve a problem.

❦

A political assembly is most in its element
when somewhat disassembled.

❦

Few investments provide a better risk-reward
ratio than a well-placed political contribution.

❦

It is the province of democratic government
not so much to create opportunity
as to restrain its denial.

❦

Opportunity rationalizes inequity.

The wheels of democracy grind slowly,
commonly enabling effective regulation
of an emerging industry only after the initial
waves of exploitation have occurred
and valuable prerogatives are firmly in place.

❦

Chance: the last resort of equity.

❦

Those most disposed to curtail the freedom of
others are those — whatever their
apparent circumstances — whose psyches
have kept them from having felt
or desired it keenly themselves.

❦

Many who proclaim that life is not fair
seem compelled to ensure it.

We tolerate injustice for its drama.

⁙

We tolerate adversity to honor overcoming it.

⁙

Social justice could be easily accomplished
if everyone contributed ratably.

⁙

Many a passion for social justice
is absorbed by the minor arts.

⁙

The world is conspicuously divided
between those who view adversity
as primarily the cause of people's failings and
those who view it primarily as the result of them.

America is a harsh culture
encompassing a multitude of benign ones.

⚜

Among rationales offered for economic
or social stratification, merit has the advantage
of the greatest following among those
best qualified to challenge it.

⚜

Many who most disparage government
are among the quickest to exploit it.

⚜

Government is democracy's whipping boy.

⚜

If you want to do something unpopular,
enlist the government to require it.

The rights of a citizen tend to be well defined
and zealously enforced, the responsibilities
vague and mostly voluntary.

❧

Bureaucracy: a place where one person's passions
collide with another's procedures.

❧

Democracy tolerates powerful appellate judges
because the lifestyle is unappealing to tyrants.

❧

Advocates of war are emboldened
by the randomness of its casualties.

❧

Each day of honorable peace
is a triumph of statesmanship.

Taxes give government a bad name.

❦

With a large enough tax base, a nation
can occasionally afford to do the right thing.

❦

Tax policy tends to be effected
less through the application of principles
than through the marshaling and disposition
of exceptions to them.

❦

Compliance with tax laws is furthered
either by simplicity or by sufficient complexity
to ensure the involvement of professionals.
The former having been long ago abandoned,
the latter has become of convienence
and necessity a staple of tax legislation.

Taxation is the primal political act,
the tax break the primal political favor.

⚜

Tax break:
a subsidy masquerading as capitalism.

⚜

You won't go to jail for not paying
the debts of your parents, but might for
not paying the debts of your parents' Congress.

⚜

Tax code:
the fine print of the social contract.

⚜

Reputation

Reputation:
the crowning achievement of hearsay.

Reputation:
a substitute of an imperfect world for truth.

A favorable reputation is at once among the most
prized and least reliable of assessments.

One is only as important
as the sum of others' opinions.

❧

Reputations are the mortar of a power structure.

❧

The more reliant one is on reputation,
the more apt to conform.

❧

The public are sufficiently skeptical to avoid
believing something unless it's at least half true.

❧

Appearances are deceiving
just often enough to continue to be so.

❧

The exalted stand on the shoulders
of the productive.

❦

Publisher: an instrumentality
for converting fame into fortune.

❦

Nothing humanizes like an obituary.

❦

The Sexes

There are many lovely women, young man,
but only one of you.

❧

Turning one's head may be a harbinger
of many contortions to come.

❧

It's better to have loved and lost
than never to have loved at all,
especially if you enjoy living in the past.

Take up with a person who boasts of getting
what he wants at the risk of being had.

⚜

Exclusive romantic relationship:
a condition for which a talent to commence
fuels an incentive to conclude.

⚜

A healthy romance beats a host
of arguments won.

⚜

The battle of the sexes
is best fought in skirmishes —
and preferably by mercenaries.

⚜

Even with our consciousnesses raised about
the prevalence of similarities between the sexes
and about guarding against exploitation
and violence between them,
of the available descriptive options,
we commonly choose to characterize them
as "opposite."

⊱⊰

Courtship: one of life's few endeavors that
routinely favors earnestness over experience.

⊱⊰

Courtship: a game commonly played
by amateurs for professional stakes.

⊱⊰

Chivalry died of a broken heart.

⊱⊰

Many a person becomes more set in his ways
when he contemplates becoming set in another's.

❧

Most successful marriages are of a type
Hollywood would have preempted
through a last-minute romantic intervention.

❧

The most consequential
voluntarily adopted phrase in the
English language: "forsaking all others."

❧

Marriage: a contract for which most of the
negotiations are held after the deal is made.

❧

The Social Arena at Large

The best or worst feature
of most lives is the company.

⚜

In the land of the blind,
the one-eyed man is king. In the land of
one-eyed men, the two-eyed man is a freak.

Walk with a tread
that portends the stick you carry.

❧

Many a bark is to avoid being bitten.

❧

Those who live by the sword die by the sword.
Just stay out of the way in the meantime.

❧

Mutually assured destruction:
a dominant principle of coexistence
since the beginning of animosity.

❧

Recluse's lament:
so much to avoid, so little time to avoid it.

Misplaced fences make bad neighbors.

Good fences make good neighbors.
Good walls make bad ones.

Without comparisons there are no disabilities.

What we most fear
happens daily to countless others.

Advice is more commonly heeded than sought.

Silence is acquiescence only to the talkative.

Sound advice:
that regarding which no hard feelings
are incurred for not heeding.

❧

Most who think they're above the fray
are actually just off to the side.

❧

Conversation: a bridge between souls.

❧

The garrulous have answers
for which there are no questions.

❧

Bad conversation drives out good.

❧

The failing of the dull is to talk
when they should listen; of the bright,
to listen when they should talk.

❧

Good listeners are made by bad ones.

❧

Personal space: the region within which
differences of opinion are expressed
between baseball managers and umpires.

❧

A barb aimed at a loved one will prick oneself.

❧

A friend supports; a good friend enhances.

❧

A friend will help you get what you want;
a good friend will help you decide what that is.

∗

One good relationship commonly begets another.

∗

Enjoying the successes of others
multiplies one's opportunities for happiness.

∗

Achieving happiness most commonly
lies in creating conditions through which
others will bring one happiness.

∗

A talent for attracting people
produces half a social life.

To bring others in you must put yourself out.

❧

To begin a friendship, show your strengths;
to seal it, show your foibles.

❧

Beware a person with no old friends —
or only old friends.

❧

The best of friends were strangers once.

❧

If you would be a friend of all,
you must take an interest in all — one by one.

❧

It's often difficult to be considered thoughtful without the help of someone considered nosy.

⁕

Blemishes fade with exposure.

⁕

The opposite of loving may be ignoring rather than hating, but most people would rather be ignored than hated.

⁕

Companionship is the province of the genuinely personable, advancement that of the politically personable.

⁕

Obligations make the world go 'round.

It is a rare person
unable to make useful introductions.

❧

People have a natural inclination
to be with people made up to be like themselves.

❧

Party: a series of encounters
enlivened by the prospect of interruption.

❧

Social pressure: a means of converting
a convenience into an imperative.

❧

There's more to winning over a group
than winning over its members.

Most people of privilege
require it for a sense of belonging.

⚜

The best induction
is in the nature of a ratification.

⚜

People tend to be less fearful
of people different from themselves
than of cultures different from their own.

⚜

Even the devil has friends.

⚜

The most private are the least informed.

⚜

Anyone who thinks he can do without others
has reason to believe he'll need to.

❧

Loyalty: a virtue that spawns many vices.

❧

The hardest to like
are the least needy and the most needy.

❧

Actions speak louder than words,
though seldom louder than feelings.

❧

There's no competition in loving,
only in being loved.

❧

Love is not being made to feel sorry
for having said you're sorry.

❧

Namelessness and facelessness
are in the eye of the beholder.

❧

There are no ordinary people,
just ordinary observations of people.

❧

A kindness from a friend builds trust in her;
from a stranger, trust in humankind.

❧

Work

The economy is society's power source,
employment the principal means of tapping it.

❧

Nearly every great work
proceeds from a need to earn a living.

❧

A person usually enjoys doing what she does well —
unless she insists on doing everything well.

Any job is impossible
if you're thorough enough.

⚜

Many a qualification for one calling
is a handicap for another.

⚜

A generalist is overqualified
for any job she can do.

⚜

A generalist is a specialist in generalities.

⚜

The more varied one's talents,
the more unused most of the time.

⚜

A youth culture is nurtured
by a society seeking subordinates.

❦

The stuff of potential
is more malleable than that of experience.

❦

As long as nearly no one is indispensable,
nearly everyone will conform.

❦

Qualification for an occupation
is commonly based
on what you learned at school.
Success in it is more often based
on what you learned at home.

❦

Schooling at best teaches how to do a job.
Experience teaches how to survive in it.

❧

Job security:
the bane of the unemployed and underemployed.

❧

As soon as people determined
they wanted more than just
livelihoods from their jobs,
it was inevitable there wouldn't
be enough of them.

❧

Jobs will be scarce as long as
the average person expects
more than the average job.

❧

It's in the interest of nearly every happily
employed person that the employment market
be at least a little bit flawed.

❧

Unemployment as a characteristic of the labor
force: a chronic condition commonly treated
as an aberration.

❧

Unemployment: the economy's form of hazing.

❧

Unemployment: a plague from which
the afflicted are expected to heal themselves.

❧

The safety net of the employment system
is desperation.

The unemployed are a just small enough
proportion of the workforce
to enable the chronically employed
and their dependents to believe that
anyone who wants a good job can get one.

❦

Nepotism:
a triumph of family values.

❦

Many a reputed old-boy network
suffers from faulty connections.

❦

Hidden job market:
the difference between what capitalism
promises to most workers and what it delivers.

❦

Endeavor: one of multiple
unspecified activities anticipated to be
engaged in at some future time
by a person currently undergoing
a career transition.

❧

Many an onerous task is accomplished
in avoidance of another more so.

❧

A tedious task is best deferred
until the mind is full.

❧

A trait likely to aid promotion
to a more elite league often hinders
advancement within a current one.

❧

A deadline demands that a job be done —
and not overdone.

⚜

Personal computer: a device
for transforming a clerk into an executive
and an executive into a clerk.

⚜

Technology allows people
to spend more time with their families,
who are increasingly the only people they know.

⚜

If you need a job done,
ask a busy person —
he's less likely to let his own needs interfere.

⚜

Those for whom time is money
tend to substitute money for time.

⁂

Overwork impairs
what recreation it doesn't preempt.

⁂

A workaholic makes work of play.

⁂

He who pours his soul into his work
pours his work into his soul.

⁂

The world of work has two tracks:
one to prosper, the other to survive.

⁂

A livelihood is a necessity,
a particular livelihood a privilege.

❧

The optimum career pays you
to be what you already are.

❧

An extraordinary career
requires an extraordinary constituency.

❧

Passion sustains a career;
intensity drains it.

❧

Hard work seldom hurts anyone
as much as does the absence of what it preempts.

There is no necessary correlation
between what you want to do for a living
and what others are willing to pay for.

❧

A successful career is one that progressively
diminishes the competition for one's services.

❧

A successful circuitous career is often envied,
rarely replicated.

❧

The primary qualification for most good jobs
is incumbency.

❧

One spouse's career tends to nurture the other's.

Within no other occupation is the compensation
as varied as in that of homemaker.

❧

Salary survey:
a study prone to understating risks
and stresses of positions other than those
to which the results will be applied.

❧

Little wonder at the American propensity
to pay executives disproportionately to the rank
and file: the precedent was set with Columbus.

❧

We pay lip service to sacrifice
but commonly pay the most to people
whose jobs are inherently satisfying.

❧

Many a tentacle of evil is supplied by a hireling.

❧

An entrepreneur learns what she wills,
a professional what she must.

❧

Management: a function of the necessity
that someone unencumbered by the demands of
doing a job is available to see that it gets done.

❧

One who sells services by the hour
can't afford obsessions.

❧

As a profession becomes more crowded,
its subject matter becomes more complicated.

Professionalism entails both knowing a lot
and feeling comfortable not knowing a lot.

A profession thrives on its rigors.

Retirement:
a time for learning a host of things
that would have been useful earlier.

Index

Captive Notions

Captive Notions

Captive Notions

Captive Notions

Captive Notions

164

Captive Notions

About the Author

John King is a native and resident of the Seattle area. A lawyer in private practice, his career has included service as a Navy judge advocate, special counsel to a U.S. Senate committee, and a law school adjunct professor. He has also been a CPA and has held positions in business. He is a graduate of Princeton, the Harvard Law School, and the University of Florida, Levin College of Law, Graduate Program in Taxation.

Mr. King has been for many years active in an Episcopal church and — now in his seventh decade — continues a nearly lifelong recreational pastime of full-court basketball. He has three grown children.

To Order Additional Copies

You may order additional copies of

CAPTIVE NOTIONS:
Concise Commentaries
on the Commonplace

at

www.captivenotions.com

or from

Pathway Book Service
4 White Brook Road
Gilsum, NH 03448
Telephone: 800-345-6665
Facsimile: 603-357-2073
Website: www.pathwaybook.com
E-mail address: pbs@pathwaybook.com